I0159739

Ptime Flies
Like A
Pterodactyl

— a Kranky Kids® play —

Ptime Flies Like A Pterodactyl

A Short Play of 22 Scenes
by
Lishka DeVoss

Copyright ©2023 Lishka DeVoss/Kranky Kids®
All rights reserved.

ISBN:
978-1-63441-019-9

ACKNOWLEDGMENTS

For the original Kranky Kids

Published
by
Toad & Fox

Using These Scripts

Various versions of these scripts are available for free on the Kranky Kids website. Yes, that means you can download these scripts individually and read them aloud in class. You can also watch and listen to performances of them.

In this book, lines are formatted and punctuated to enhance:

- ease of reading and memorization
- working with partners
- keeping track on the page
- developing a pace/tempo for line delivery
- general note-taking

Make these scripts work for you. For example, **Cave Hollywood** has a lot of spoof names of movies and books that were current when we did live productions. Make up your own spoof names of more recent films or get rid of any you don't like.

Most of these skits work for both live theater and radio/podcast.

Kranky Kids® Script Use/Reuse Notice

Educators have permission to use Lishka DeVoss/Kranky Kids® copyrighted scripts in productions under the following three conditions:

1. You must first contact Kranky Kids at *krankykids.com* and get permission.

2. You must give credit to Kranky Kids during your production and performance and also in any printed or digital material related to your production/performance (posters, newsletters, programs, flyers, etc).

3. All profits made from your production/performance must be applied only to one or more of the following:

- funding a school's drama department
- funding a school's tech/video department
- funding an after-school program
- giving a party for the students who have participated in the production

Please respect these conditions and give credit to Kranky Kids when it's due. A lot of hard work has gone into producing these scripts. Thank you.

CONTENTS

CONTENTS

There are twenty-two (22) scenes in this play and it lasts about an hour. It was written for a cast of seven; all the roles are interchangeable. This play can also be used for a large group of students by assigning one scene to each student (which has the added benefit of less complaints about learning so many lines).

Our costumes consisted of all-blackish underclothing covered by fake-fur ponchos belted at the waist (usually in the front only). Ponchos with jagged-edges were decorated with large wooden beads that slid over cut strips — creating a fun primitive-looking fringe. The fake fur designs from the local fabric store that we used were cheetah, tiger, brown bear and black-and-white cow.

Spears were made using wooden dowels (3-feet long, ½-inch thick) wrapped in red-colored duct tape and decorated with fake feathers made of felt that were attached to several different lengths of thin braided multi-colored plastic strands. The braided strands were tied to one end of each spear with the feathers left dangling. For safety reasons and because kids will be kids, the spears had no sharp heads.

Seven dinosaur hobbyhorses were used. The somewhat flat dinosaur heads were made from foam core covered with paper mache and tempera paint, then sealed with a plastic spray. The heads were attached to dowels which were then wrapped with various colored duct tape (blue, green and red). Two lengths of colored chiffon (2-feet by 4-feet each) were attached to the base of each head with the longest corners knotted together at the other end.

The actors, when carrying a head, would drape the chiffon over their shoulders (with the knot placed at the back of their neck) causing the loose fabric to hang and flow like a pair of fat decorative reins on a horse. Specific dinosaurs were chosen for their unique head shapes so as to make them more individual to the audience from a distance.

During the entire production, an easel stood far over to one side (downstage left) holding individual poster boards with the name of each scene lettered large upon them for the audience to read.

To simplify reproducing this play, in the following section all the scenes are listed by number and name with their characters, props and sound effects (SFX) for use by the director and cast (who act as their own stage hands). Incidental music was played between each scene to give the actors time for each set-up. Find and/or compose your own music for your performance.

To see and hear some of our performances of this play and also to have a look at what our original costumes and props looked like, go to: krankykids.com (and look under DRAMA and INFO).

CHARACTERS, PROPS, SFX

SCENE 1: THE INVENTION OF POPCORN

CHARACTERS:

POCORN HANDLER: Introduces popcorn to CAVE PEOPLE.

CAVE PEOPLE: The rest of the cast except POPCORN HANDLER.

PROPS:
1. a fake fire painted on foam core and attached to a box

2. a metal skillet that sits on top of the box behind the fake fire
3. unpopped popcorn kernels in a drawstring bag
4. a bag of unopened already-popped microwave popcorn in the open part of the box below where the skillet sits
5. poster board on easel reading: **The Invention of Popcorn**

SFX:
1. single pops and then lots of loud pops sounding all at once
2. incidental music

SCENE 2: CAVE ORNITHOLOGIST

CHARACTERS:

INTERVIEWER: Reporter for the Continuous Caveman Coverage (CCC) network.

ORNITHOLOGIST: Studies birds and moves a bit like a bird. Acts nervous.

PROPS:

1. a small round table covered with a dark blue tablecloth that reaches the floor
2. a small stegosaurus made from foam core, brightly painted with the letters **CCC** on its side

Small cups filled with sand were attached on the back and then covered with paper mache before being painted so that it would stay standing on the tabletop.

3. two (2) chairs
4. poster board on easel reading: **Cave Ornithologist**

SFX:

1. bird screeches
2. CCC Theme Song
3. incidental music

SCENE 3: THE MISSING LINK 1

CHARACTERS:

FIGHTER ONE: Actor with long hair.

FIGHTER TWO: Actor with long hair.

REFEREE: Actor with whistle.

PROPS:

1. two (2) spears
2. two (2) hair scrunchies
3. a referee whistle
4. poster board on easel reading: **The Missing Link**

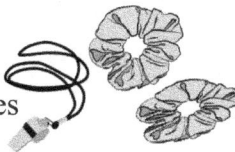

SFX: incidental music

SCENE 4: CAVE CHOIR

CHARACTERS:

INTERVIEWER: Reporter for the Continuous Caveman Coverage (CCC) network.

CHEEBO: Directs the cave choir.

CHOIR: The rest of the cast except CHEEBO and INTERVIEWER.

PROPS: poster board on easel reading: **Cave Choir**

SFX:
1. CCC Theme Song
2. incidental music

SCENE 5: THE INVENTION OF S'MORES

CHARACTERS:

NARRATOR: Tells the story of The Invention of S'mores.

CHOCOLASAURUS: Actor in dark colors.

MARSHMALLOWAPOLUS: Actor in light colors.

GRAHAM CRACKERACERATOP 1: Actor wearing a sandwich board that looks like two giant graham crackers.

GRAHAM CRACKERACERATOP 2: Actor wearing a sandwich board that looks like two giant graham crackers.

T-REX: Actor dressed in dark colors who can burp on cue consistently.

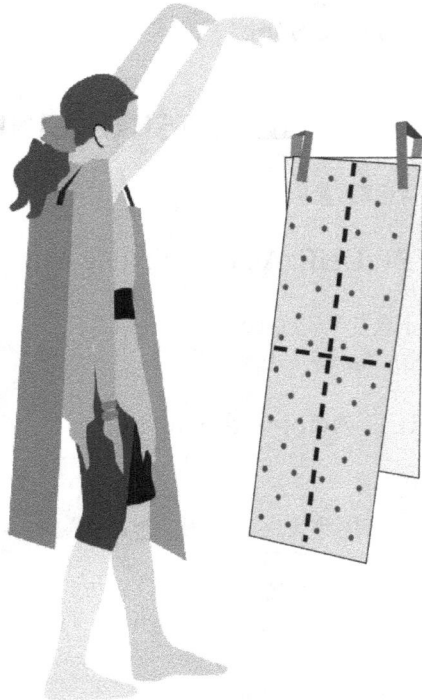

PROPS:
1. two (2) sets of sandwich boards made to look like giant graham crackers (cardboard covered with dots and creases drawn with permanent marker; 2-inch belting attached at the shoulders)
2. poster board on easel reading: **The Invention of S'mores**

SFX:
1. keyboard music
2. incidental music

SCENE 6: CAVE NUTRITIONIST

CHARACTERS:

INTERVIEWER: Reporter for the Continuous Caveman Coverage (CCC) network.

NUTRITIONIST: Studies various foods. Acts a bit spaced.

PROPS:
1. a small round table covered with a dark blue tablecloth that reaches the floor
2. a small stegosaurus made from foam core, brightly painted with the letters **CCC** on its side
3. two (2) chairs
4. poster board on easel reading: **Cave Nutritionist**

SFX:
1. CCC Theme Song
2. incidental music

SCENE 7: THE MISSING LINK 2

CHARACTERS:

ONE: Actor.

TWO: Actor.

THREE: Gives TWO a flower.

PROPS:
1. a large fake flower with a long stem
2. poster board on easel reading: **The Missing Link**

SFX: incidental music

SCENE 8: CAVE HOLLYWOOD

CHARACTERS:

INTERVIEWER: Reporter for the Continuous Caveman Coverage (CCC) network.

STONE: Famous film director.

AGTITE: Film actor who feels overlooked.

PROPS:
1. a small round table covered with a dark blue tablecloth that reaches the floor
2. a small stegosaurus made from foam core, brightly painted with the letters **CCC** on its side
3. three (3) chairs
4. poster board on easel reading: **Cave Hollywood**

SFX:
1. CCC Theme Song
2. incidental music

SCENE 9: GIFTS OF THE PALEOZOIC

CHARACTERS:

TEACHER: Leads a class in explaining natural resources discovered during the Paleozoic Era.

COAL: Introduces coal as a resource.

PETRO: Introduces petroleum as a resource.

SALT: Introduces salt as a resource.

STONE: Introduces limestone as a resource.

PROPS:
1. a small notepad and pencil
2. poster board on easel reading: **Gifts of The Paleozoic**

SFX: incidental music

SCENE 10: CAVE CIRCUS TRAINER

CHARACTERS:

INTERVIEWER: Reporter for the Continuous Caveman Coverage (CCC) network.

TRAINER: Gruff and rough sounding.

BROTHER: Acts and sounds like a goofy animal.

PROPS:
1. a small round table covered with a dark blue tablecloth that reaches the floor
2. a small stegosaurus made from foam core, brightly painted with the letters **CCC** on its side
3. two (2) chairs
4. poster board on easel reading: **Cave Circus Trainer**

SFX:
1. CCC Theme Song
2. incidental music

SCENE 11: CAVE DRILL SQUAD

CHARACTERS:

SQUAD 1: Actor.

SQUAD 2: Actor.

SQUAD 3: Actor.

SQUAD 4: Actor.

SQUAD 5: Actor.

SQUAD 6: Actor.

SQUAD 7: Actor.

PROPS:
1. seven (7) spears, one for each actor
2. poster board on easel reading: **Cave Drill Squad**

SFX: incidental music

SCENE 12: THE MISSING LINK 3

CHARACTERS:

GROUP ONE: Three actors.

GROUP TWO: Three actors.

TV HANDLER: Brings out the TV.

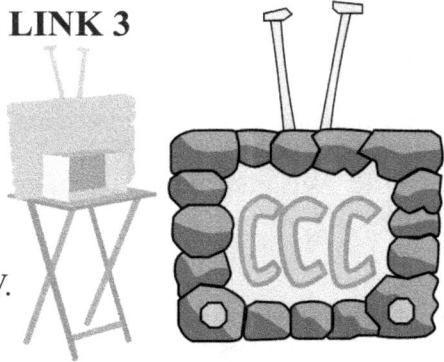

PROPS:
1. a Stone Age TV made of foam core (with the letters **CCC** in the middle of the screen) attached to the side of a box
2. a tray stand
3. poster board on easel reading: **The Missing Link**

SFX: incidental music

SCENE 13: ICE AGE PIZZA

CHARACTERS:

SMILODONE: Enthusiastic pizza shop co-owner.

SCIMITAR: Enthusiastic pizza shop co-owner.

NEANDERTHAL ONE: Ear-pickin' dumb-lookin' pizza delivery kid.

NEANDERTHAL TWO: Butt-scratchin' dumb-lookin' pizza delivery kid.

PROPS:
1. two (2) tall puffy chef hats
2. a small round table covered with a red-and-white checkered tablecloth that reaches the floor
3. a big tall cup that reads **Triassic Tumbler** on the side
4. a big squat cup that reads **Jurassic Jelly Jar** on the side

5. a green two-liter soda bottle that reads **Stone Age Soda** on the label
6. fake large flat green ginkgo leaves on a long stem
7. two (2) empty pizza boxes with **Ice Age Pizza** on the top of each box (slots are cut out underneath to allow the delivery kids to hold and tip the boxes so the audience can read the business name)
8. poster board on easel reading: **Ice Age Pizza**

SFX: incidental music

SCENE 14: CAVE TRIATHLON

CHARACTERS:

HUSBAND: Triathlete who isn't too bright.

WIFE: Frustrated wife of triathlete.

FRIEND: Friend of wife who sympathizes with her dilemma.

PROPS: poster board on easel reading: **Cave Triathlon**

SFX: incidental music

SCENE 15: MEASURING DINOSAURS

CHARACTERS:

INTERVIEWER: Reporter for the Continuous Caveman Coverage (CCC) network.

PROFESSOR: Acts goofy and wears big glasses. (If the actor also has braces it's a plus!)

PROPS:
1. a small round table covered with a dark blue tablecloth that reaches the floor

2. a small stegosaurus made from foam core, brightly painted with the letters **CCC** on its side
3. two (2) chairs
4. a pair of large glasses
5. poster board on easel reading: **Measuring Dinosaurs**

SFX:
1. CCC Theme Song
2. incidental music

SCENE 16: DINOSAUR SURGERY

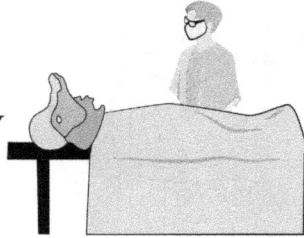

CHARACTERS:

PATIENT: Dinosaur being operated on.

MOTHER: Stoic and getting annoyed.

FATHER: Weepy and semi-hysterical.

SURGEON ONE: Very serious and straight-forward.

SURGEON TWO: Very empathic and sympathetic.

SURGEON THREE: Show-off.

SURGEON FOUR: Has a cold.

PROPS:
1. a plank over two (2) crates or a small bench
2. a white sheet that covers the PATIENT and reaches to the floor on three sides
3. two (2) chairs
4. four (4) sets of surgical gloves and masks (for the surgeons)
5. box that sits behind PATIENT with the following inside:
- a depiction of Atlantis painted on foam core
- a pair of tennis shoes
- a small skateboard
- a bag of cookies
6. poster board on easel reading: **Dinosaur Surgery**

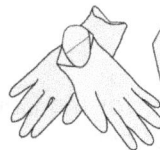

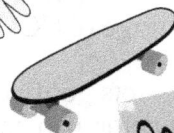

SFX: incidental music

SCENE 17: DINOSAUR MINUETTE

CHARACTERS: Each actor holds a dinosaur hobbyhorse in front on them and places the lower knot at the back of their neck; this lets the fabric hang and flow over their shoulders like a pair of fat decorative reins on a horse. They hold the dinosaur heads high in the air while dancing.

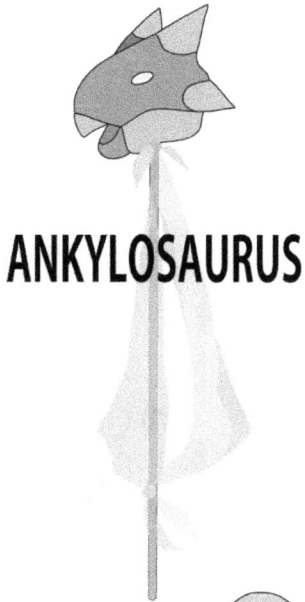

ANKYLOSAURUS

CHASMOSAURUS

CORYTHOSAURUS

DILOPHOSAURUS

PARASAUROLOPHUS

TYRANNOSAURUS REX

PROTOCERATOPS

Dinosaur Minuette

PROPS:
1. seven (7) different dinosaur hobbyhorses made from foam core covered with paper mache and tempra paint, then sealed with a plastic spray. Dowels are wrapped with colored duct tape and two lengths of colored chiffon (2-feet by 4-feet each) are attached to the base of each head with the longest corners knotted together at the other end.
2. poster board on easel reading: **Dinosaur Minuette**

SFX: Bach's Minuette in G

SCENE 18: CAVE FASHION DESIGNER

CHARACTERS:

INTERVIEWER: Reporter for the Continuous Caveman Coverage (CCC) network.

FABRICO: Flamboyant, over-the-top designer with a long showy scarf.

PROPS:
1. a small round table covered with a dark blue tablecloth that reaches the floor
2. a small stegosaurus made from foam core, brightly painted with the letters **CCC** on its side
3. two (2) chairs
4. poster board on easel reading: **Cave Fashion Designer**

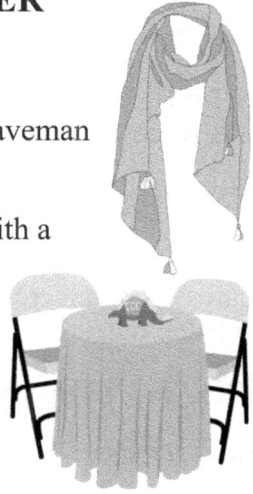

SFX:
1. CCC Theme Song
2. incidental music

SCENE 19: THE MISSING LINK 4

CHARACTERS:

ONE: Rock lifter.

TWO: Rock lifter.

THREE: Rock lifter.

PROPS:
1. a fake boulder made from wadded-up paper or packing peanuts inside a large garbage bag that is inside a grey cloth bag that has been painted to look rock-like
2. poster board on easel reading: **The Missing Link**

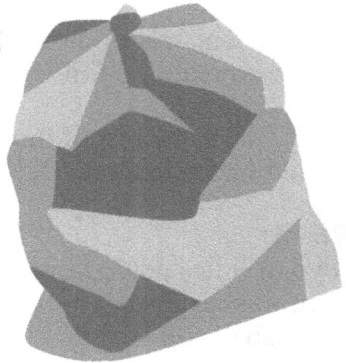

SFX: incidental music

SCENE 20: CAVE ARTIST

CHARACTERS:

INTERVIEWER: Reporter for the Continuous Caveman Coverage (CCC) network.

DOUBLE HELIX: Over-the-top egotistical artist who makes big gestures when speaking.

PROPS: poster board on easel reading: **Cave Artist**

SFX:
1. progressive thunderous rumbling sounds
2. incidental music

SCENE 21: THE INVENTION OF CHOWDER

CHARACTERS:

TUNIC: Sports anchor holding a fake mic.

SANDAL: Sports anchor holding a fake mic.

REFEREE: Official with a cap on and wearing a whistle.

CHOWS: The rest of the cast with signs in their right hands reading: **CHOW**.

DERS: The same rest of the cast with signs in their left hands reading: **DER**.

PROPS:
1. two (2) mics made from wooden spoons or hairbrushes
2. a baseball cap
3. a referee whistle
4. four (4) small signs on sticks reading **CHOW** on both sides
5. four (4) small signs on sticks reading **DER** on both sides
6. poster board on easel reading: **The Invention of Chowder**

SFX:
1. generic crowd sounds
2. splashing sounds
3. whistle blowing
4. incidental music

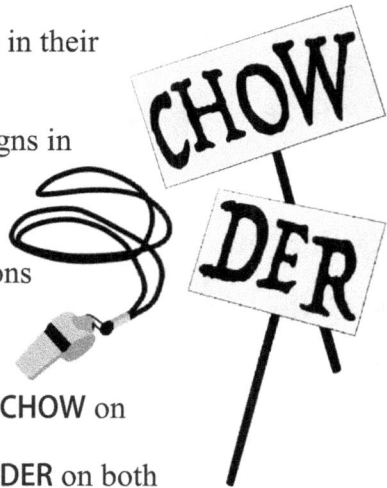

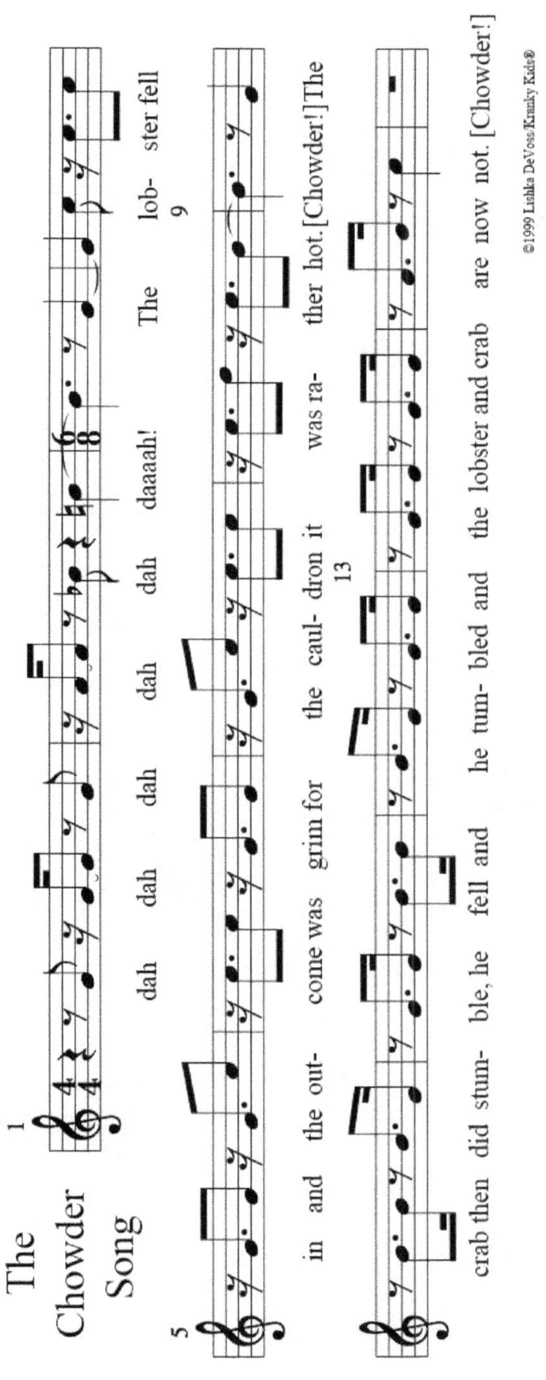
The Chowder Song
dah dah dah dah dah dah daaaah! The lob- ster fell
in and the out- come was grim for the caul- dron it was ra- ther hot. [Chowder!] The
crab then did stum- ble, he fell and he tum- bled and the lobster and crab are now not. [Chowder!]
©1999 Lishka DeVoss/Kranky Kids®

SCENE 22: THE EXTINCTION OF DINOSAURS

CHARACTERS: Each actor holds a dinosaur hobbyhorse in front their face.

ANKYLOSAURUS: see Scene 17

CHASMOSAURUS: see Scene 17

CORYTHOSAURUS: see Scene 17

DILOPHOSAURUS: see Scene 17

PARASAUROLOPHUS: see Scene 17

PROTOCERATOPS: see Scene 17

TYRANNOSAURUS REX: see Scene 17

PROPS:
1. seven (7) dinosaur hobbyhorses
2. seven (7) travel bottles of mouthwash
2. poster board on easel reading:
The Extinction of Dinosaurs

SFX: incidental music

Scene 1 - The Invention of Popcorn

SETTING:
A fake fire sits on the ground rear center stage. An easel standing far
downstage left holds individual poster boards with the name of each
scene in their order of production. The easel remains on stage for the
entire play.

AT RISE:
Poster board on easel reads: The Invention of Popcorn.

(*While making grumbling noises, CAVE PEOPLE and POPCORN
HANDLER enter from both sides of the stage and then sit around the fire.
Some have their backs to the audience.*)

(*POPCORN HANDLER eventually moves to sit behind the fire and faces
the audience. Makes grunting noises while sitting up on knees, holding up
a drawstring cloth bag and pointing to it. Takes some kernels out of the
bag and holds them out for CAVE PEOPLE to see.*)

(*CAVE PEOPLE all grunt in interest at the bag and kernels.*)

(*POPCORN HANDLER with exaggerated gestures loudly drops the
kernels into the pan behind the fire.*)

(*POPCORN HANDLER and CAVE PEOPLE all move in closer while
making grunting noises and lean into the fire with even greater interest.*)

SFX: a loud pop

(*Everyone scoots back a bit, looking fearful.*)

SFX: a loud pop

(*Everyone scoots back even further while acting even more alarmed.*)

SFX: a whole bunch of really loud popping sounds

(*Everyone jumps up and runs offstage in various directions — even into
the audience aisles if it's a theater-in-the-round situation — while making
"I'm scared" noises. When the popping sounds stop, everyone cautiously
gathers back around the fire.*)

(POPCORN HANDLER returns to position behind the fire, pulls out the bag of microwave popcorn and holds it up, looking confused.)

POPCORN HANDLER : Huuuuh?

(Blackout and end of Scene 1.)

SFX: incidental music

Scene 2 - Cave Ornithologist

NOTE: Hooded Pitohui (pronounced pee-toh-HUU-ee) - There really is such a bird, I kid you not, and it really is poisonous.
NOTE: grebes (pronounced GREHBS) - various swimming and diving birds.
NOTE: barbets (pronounced BAHR-bihts) - various brightly colored tropical birds related to the toucan.

SETTING:
INTERVIEWER and ORNITHOLOGIST are both seated downstage right at a table with the CCC stegosaurus as the centerpiece.

AT RISE:
Poster board on easel reads: Cave Ornithologist

INTERVIEWER :   Today we have with us the Cave Clan's resident ornithologist.

What got you interested in studying birds?

ORNITHOLOGIST : Fear.

INTERVIEWER :   You're afraid of them?

ORNITHOLOGIST : Oh yes, very much so.

Razor sharp beaks to peck your eyes out, claws that can rip you to shreds.

You can never be too wary of our feathered friends.

INTERVIEWER :   But don't you have to get close to the birds you're studying?

ORNITHOLOGIST : Absolutely.

However, I've discovered a guaranteed method of scaring them off if they get too close or even look like they're going to attack.

It's the call of the Ancient Trogon.

ORNITHOLOGIST
(cont.) :   Would you like me to demonstrate?

INTERVIEWER :   Please do.

SFX: bird screech
(*ORNITHOLOGIST either mimes the call while it's piped in on the
stage sound system or actually lets out a horrible loud cawing sound
and INTERVIEWER covers ears and winces.*)

ORNITHOLOGIST : Would you like to hear it again?

INTERVIEWER :   Oh, please, no!

                            That was awful.

                            How did you discover this call?

ORNITHOLOGIST : Ah, now that's an excellent question.

                            One day, I was following a flock of fancy
flamingos on their daily trot through the bogs
when all of a sudden I heard this cry and
WHOOSH!

                            Up went the flamingos and every other bird in
the bog.

                            It was a madhouse.

                            All that was left was this tiny little puff of a
creature, no bigger than my palm.

INTERVIEWER :   And that was a Trogon?

ORNITHOLOGIST : Absolutely.

                            I believe they are a direct descendent of the
Giant Pterodactyl.

                            But I've never been able to catch one, you see.

INTERVIEWER :   Because they're so fast?

ORNITHOLOGIST : Oh no, no, no, no, no!

Because I'd probably go deaf.

They're so LOUD!

SFX: bird screech
(*ORNITHOLOGIST again either mimes the call or actually lets out a horrible loud cawing sound and INTERVIEWER covers ears and winces.*)

INTERVIEWER :   Hey hey hey!

Please!

I get your point!

ORNITHOLOGIST : Sorry about that.

I get a little carried away.

INTERVIEWER :   What are your favorite birds to study?

ORNITHOLOGIST : Well, let's see now.

That would have to be grebes and barbets.

Oh, and let us not forget the Hooded Pitohui.

It's poisonous, you know.

INTERVIEWER :   Really.

ORNITHOLOGIST : Yes, very poisonous.

Just gave one to a friend the other day.

We had a little fight, you see.

So I thought I'd make amends with the gift of a Hooded Pitohui.

INTERVIEWER :   And did your friend like it?

ORNITHOLOGIST :
(*becoming dreamy and distracted*)

> Oh, yes, very much so.
>
> Right up until he began to stiffen and lose consciousness.
>
> Terribly sad.
>
> Terribly.

SFX: CCC Theme Song plays softly

INTERVIEWER :
(*alarmed and starting to back away*)

> So sorry to hear.
>
> This is King Fisher for the CCC - Continuous Caveman Coverage.

(*Blackout and end of Scene 2.*)

SFX: incidental music

Scene 3 - The Missing Link 1

SETTING:
A blank stage with FIGHTER ONE center stage right and FIGHTER TWO center stage left, facing each other, each ready to fight holding a spear and their hair is covering their faces making it hard for them to see.

AT RISE:
Poster board on easel reads: The Missing Link

(FIGHTER ONE and FIGHTER TWO start lunging at each other, completely missing each other each time they try. They turn and cross paths on the stage each time they lunge and miss — staying relatively center stage the entire time.)

(REFEREE enters upstage left and grabs FIGHTER ONE and FIGHTER TWO each by the shoulder. They stand still while REFEREE hands them each a scrunchie.)

(FIGHTER ONE and FIGHTER TWO make a big production out of pulling their hair back and keeping it in place with the scrunchie. Now they can see each other.)

(FIGHTER ONE and FIGHTER TWO then stand poised, spears ready for attack.)

(REFEREE blows whistle for them to continue the fight.)

(Blackout and end of Scene 3.)

SFX: incidental music

Scene 4 - Cave Choir

SETTING:
CHOIR standing in a row center stage. INTERVIEWER and CHEEBO are standing in front of them.

AT RISE:
Poster board on easel reads: Cave Choir

INTERVIEWER :   Tonight we are at a performance of the Cave Choir with Cheebo conducting.

                         I understand you teach a very unique method for singing.

CHEEBO :   Yes, that's true.

                         It's a relaxation technique.

                         You have to relax the tongue —

(speaking with a relaxed tongue, i.e. leaving the tongue on the bottom of the mouth and not making any distinct consonants)

                         — something like this.

INTERVIEWER :
(confused)
                         Like what?

CHEEBO :
(still speaking with a relaxed tongue)

                         Like this.

(speaking normally again)

                         You see it is much easier to sing when you don't have your tongue wagging about and in the way.

                         All those consonants in our language just interfere with the smooth production of sound.

CHEEBO
(cont.) :   All song sings on vowels, you know.

INTERVIEWER :   I see you have your choir primed and ready to
                             start.

                             Shall we have a demonstration performance?

CHEEBO :   By all means —

(*begins conducting in 4/4 time*)

                             — one, two, three, four.
CHOIR :
(*all singing with a relaxed tongue*)

                             Row row row your boat

                             Gently down the stream

                             Merrily merrily merrily merrily

(*slowing the song down and bending forward at the waist slowly while
singing the last line*)

                             Life...is...but...a...dream.

(*Like bent marionettes, CHOIR holds position.*)

CHEEBO :
(*bowing all the while*)

                             Thank you.

                             Thank you.

                             Well, what did you think?

(*CHOIR returns to upright posture.*)

INTERVIEWER :   But, but, I couldn't understand a word they were
                             saying!

CHEEBO :   Sure you can.

CHEEBO
(cont.) :

You just have to free up your mind, that's all.

Here, listen again —

(*begins conducting in 4/4 time*)

— one, two, three, four.

CHOIR
(*all singing with a relaxed tongue*)

Row row row your boat

Gently down the stream

Merrily merrily merrily merrily

(*slowing the song down and bending forward at the waist slowly while singing the last line*)

Life...is...but...a...dream.

(*Like bent marionettes, CHOIR holds position.*)

CHEEBO :
(*bowing all the while*)

Thank you.

Thank you.

You see?

Did you understand better this time?

INTERVIEWER :

Uh, um, yes, I guess so.

This is Herdit All for the CCC - Continuous Caveman Coverage.

(*Blackout and end of Scene 4.*)

SFX: incidental music

Scene 5 - The Invention of S'mores

SETTING:
Standing next to the easel stage right is NARRATOR. Center stage are MARSHMALLOWAPOLUS and CHOCOLASAURUS, facing each other. Center stage left facing offstage stands GRAHAM CRACKERACERATOP 1, center stage right facing offstage stands GRAHAM CRACKERACERATOP 2.

AT RISE:
Poster board on easel reads: The Invention of S'mores

SFX: Whimsical, light repetitive keyboard music is playing softly in the background, preferably in 4/4 time.

NARRATOR :   Once upon a time —

(*MARSHMALLOWAPOLUS and CHOCOLASAURUS pretend to throw a large beach ball back and forth to each other.*)

          — there was a baby Chocolasaurus —

(*CHOCOLASAURUS turns to the audience and either curtsies or bows, then returns to playing with MARSHMALLOWAPOLUS.*)

          — and, a baby Marshmallowapolus.

(*MARSHMALLOWAPOLUS turns to the audience and either curtsies or bows, then returns to playing with CHOCOLASAURUS.*)

          Together, they were playing in the meadow.

CHOCOLASAURUS
and
MARSHMALLOWAPOLUS :
(*singing and playing*)

          La-la-la-la-la-la-la.

NARRATOR :   Little did they know, two big —

SFX: minor chord sounds

(GRAHAM CRACKERACERATOP 1 and 2 both pivot and now face the audience.)

NARRATOR
(cont.) :   — mean —

SFX: a different higher-pitched minor chord sounds

(GRAHAM CRACKERACERATOP 1 and 2 both raise their arms and hold up their hands looking like claws at shoulder height. MARSHMALLOWAPOLUS and CHOCOLASAURUS continue playing, oblivious to the threat.)

(with emphasis)

                              — hungry —

SFX: a different even higher-pitched minor chord sounds

(GRAHAM CRACKERACERATOP 1 and 2 both pivot again to now face MARSHMALLOWAPOLUS and CHOCOLASAURUS while raising their arms above their heads, their hands still looking like claws. MARSHMALLOWAPOLUS and CHOCOLASAURUS continue playing, still oblivious to the threat.)

                              — Graham Crackeraceratops were sneaking up on them.

                              And they were —

(GRAHAM CRACKERACERATOP 1 and 2 move forward and push MARSHMALLOWAPOLUS and CHOCOLASAURUS together from both sides and wrap their arms around them, trapping them.)

                              — trapped together!

MARSHMALLOWAPOLUS
and
CHOCOLASAURUS :
(looking at the audience)

                              Oh no!

                              What s'more could happen to us?!

NARRATOR :   Along came a T-Rex —

(*Enter upstage left T-REX with arms bent, elbows tucked into their torso and hands looking like claws at shoulder height. T-REX lumbers up to the foursome standing center stage.*)

— and ate them all —

(*T-REX waves one arm over the trapped foursome and the foursome falls to the floor.*)

— in one bite.

(*T-REX burps loudly.*)

(*Blackout and end of Scene 5.*)

SFX: incidental music

Scene 6 - Cave Nutritionist

SETTING:
INTERVIEWER and NUTRITIONIST are both seated downstage right at a table with the CCC stegosaurus as a centerpiece.

AT RISE:
Poster board on easel reads: Cave Nutritionist

INTERVIEWER :   Today we are talking to Spook Thump, a nutritionist for many of the area caves.

Just how do you go about determining what we can eat?

NUTRITIONIST :   I usually go up a tree or hang over a ledge and then drop the potential food on someone else's head.

INTERVIEWER :   You mean you hit things that you think are food on someone else's head?

NUTRITIONIST :   Of course, silly.

How else can I be objective?

INTERVIEWER :   I see.

Yes, that does make sense, I suppose.

What other methods do you use?

NUTRITIONIST :   Well, many times I blow really hard on something to see if it will move, or fly away.

INTERVIEWER :   Fly like a bird?

NUTRITIONIST :   No, silly, like a spore or a seed because the next test is smelling.

I don't want to sniff something and have part of it go flying up my nose, you know.

INTERVIEWER :   Yes, yes, perfectly understandable.

When do you actually get around to eating it?

NUTRITIONIST :   First I feed the so-called food to the Giant
Armadillo.

INTERVIEWER :   The Giant Armadillo?

NUTRITIONIST :   Yes, the Giant Armadillo that I keep in my cave.

He's very good at eating things and then vomiting.

That way I can check if the food digests well or
not.

You see, in the beginning of my career, I
discovered many things that I thought we should
be able to eat, but we can't.

INTERVIEWER :   Like what?

NUTRITIONIST :   Well, like rocks, for instance.

It didn't matter if I stewed them, baked them,
boiled them or marinated them before grilling
— the Giant Armadillo threw up most of them.

Not one rock was ever digested.

INTERVIEWER :   How could you be sure?

NUTRITIONIST :   Because not all the rocks came out of just one
end of the Giant Armadillo.

INTERVIEWER :   I see.

Oh...OH!

Anyway, what has been the most surprising
discovery you've ever made?

NUTRITIONIST :   Nuts.

INTERVIEWER :   Excuse me?

Nuts?

What are nuts?

NUTRITIONIST :   Nuts look and feel like little rocks but they have stuff inside that's very tasty.

Two weeks ago, a chef from the Nether Cave found some under a tree.

Inside the cave he started throwing them against the cave wall for fun.

Some of them broke open and some of them stuck.

We call them 'walnuts'.

SFX: CCC Theme Song plays softly

INTERVIEWER :   That is fascinating.

Thank you.

This is Pookah Too for the CCC - Continuous Caveman Coverage.

(Blackout and end of Scene 6.)

SFX: incidental music

Scene 7 - The Missing Link 2

SETTING:
ONE sits with face in hands stage right, seeming to be crying. TWO stands upstage center.

AT RISE:
Poster board on easel reads: The Missing Link

(*ONE weeps loudly. TWO stands and fidgets, looking confused and frustrated.*)

(*THREE enters upstage left, hands TWO a flower and gestures towards ONE.*)

(*TWO takes flower, THREE exits upstage left.*)

(*TWO walks over to ONE and gives ONE the flower.*)

(*ONE accepts the flower and smiles at TWO.*)

(*Blackout and end of Scene 7.*)

SFX: incidental music

Scene 8 - Cave Hollywood

SETTING:
INTERVIEWER, STONE and AGTITE are all seated downstage right at a table with the CCC stegosaurus as the centerpiece.

AT RISE:
Poster board on easel reads: Cave Hollywood

INTERVIEWER :	This morning we are talking with Overblown Stone and Stella Agtite.
	Now, Mr. Stone, you began your career with "Night of the Living Mammoths", is that correct?
STONE :	Yes, yes it is.
	That was my first attempt at film.
	The horror, the horror of all those stampeding mammoths was something I knew teens would enjoy.
AGTITE :	Especially when the tribe elders got squashed.
INTERVIEWER :	And then your next film was —
STONE :	"I Know What You Did In The Last Mesozoic".
AGTITE :	Which was basically everyone running around trying to save their lives since the earth was busy rearranging itself with earthquakes, etc.
INTERVIEWER :	And this then led you to —
STONE :	"Children of the Caves".
	A mess, that one.
	A real mess.
	The children were obeying their parents, learning the proper ways of the hunt —

AGTITE :   And this just didn't ring true.

INTERVIEWER :   So you decided to do a film especially for children.

STONE :   Yes.

                     "The Secret Tar Pit".

                     It went over very well.

                     Changed my life, really.

AGTITE :   But then he started to get bored and wanted to do a serious film for adults.

STONE :   Absolutely.

                     I read as many cave walls as I could and finally decided on the most dramatic one in existence.

INTERVIEWER :   Which one was that?

AGTITE :   "To Kill A Pterodactyl".

STONE :   You know, with characters like Sloth and Boot, you just can't go wrong.

INTERVIEWER :   Yet you seem to be in a high comic phase now.

AGTITE :   Thanks to me.

                     I star in all three of his hit comedies right now: "There's Something About Neanderthals", "Austin Particles - International Caveman of Mystery" and last, but not least, "The Bogboy" with Adam Sandworm.

INTERVIEWER :   And they're all hilarious.

                     Well, thank you for your time. I'm certain our audience has enjoyed this —

SFX: CCC Theme Song plays softly

INTERVIEWER (cont.) :	— this is Arounda Corner for the CCC - Continuous Caveman Coverage.
AGTITE :	Thank you.
INTERVIEWER :	No, thank you, really.
STONE :	Well, we'd like to thank you also.
INTERVIEWER :	Well, you're welcome.
AGTITE :	Likewise, I'm sure.

(*Blackout and end of Scene 8.*)

SFX: incidental music

Scene 9 - Gifts of the Paleozoic

SETTING:
Center stage in a line facing the audience stand COAL, PETRO, SALT and STONE. TEACHER stands downstage right with a pad and pencil in hand, writing something down.

AT RISE:
Poster board on easel reads: Gifts of the Paleozoic

TEACHER :   The Paleozoic Era left some very interesting things.

COAL :   One of them was something Santa leaves in the stockings of bad boys and girls.

TEACHER :   Yes, let's see now, Santa, stockings, little brats...

PETRO :   Then there's that black gunk from the ground that runs too many cars and is in practically everything fake that we make.

TEACHER :   Icky black stuff, uh-huh...

SALT :   Another one is used to season food.

TEACHER :   A popular seasoning. Very impressive.

STONE :   And yet another supports many a roof.

TEACHER :   All these are very interesting things.

Can anyone guess what they are?

COAL :
(*singing on middle C*)

Coal —

PETRO :
(*singing on E above middle C*)

Petroleum —

SALT :
(*singing on G above middle C*)

        Salt —

STONE :
(*singing on B above middle C*)

        Building Stone!

SFX: singing stops

TEACHER :   Everyone got 'em?

             Coal, petroleum, salt and building stone.

             Pretty interesting, huh?

EVERYONE :   You betcha!

(*Blackout and end of Scene 9.*)

SFX: incidental music

Scene 10 - Cave Circus Trainer

SETTING:
INTERVIEWER and TRAINER are both seated downstage right at a
table with the CCC stegosaurus as the centerpiece.

AT RISE:
Poster board on easel reads: Cave Circus Trainer

INTERVIEWER :	Today we have a member of the Caveman Circus Caravan.
	Tar Rockaway is one of the animal trainers.
	Which animals do you train?
TRAINER :	Well, you see, when I started nobody could keep the Woolly Mammoths in a straight line.
	But I solved that problem right away.
INTERVIEWER :	How so?
TRAINER:	Big giant pits on each side of the runway.
	They had to stay on the runway or fall in.
	And Mammoths don't like taking spills, you know.
INTERVIEWER :	Digging those pits must have taken quite a long time.
TRAINER :	Yep, it did.
	Especially since we had to use our hands at first.
	About half way through some guy from another cave brought us this long stick with a paddle tied onto the end.
	He called it a 'shovel' and said it would make the digging easier.
INTERVIEWER :	And did it?

TRAINER :   Yep.

                   Except for the delays from the workers getting
                   hit in the head.

                   Half the men would start swinging and then
                   whack the other half in the head.

INTERVIEWER :   OW!

                   That would slow things up a bit.

                   What was your next task?

TRAINER :   Well, I wanted very much to train the saber-
                   tooth tigers, but you have to keep their fangs
                   polished.

                   Not that I'm afraid they'd bite me.

                   It's just that they drool so much and it gets all
                   over you and you can't get it off.

INTERVIEWER :   I see.

                   So what did you train?

TRAINER :   My younger brother.

(*BROTHER enters upstage left variously rolling around on the floor,
squatting and waving his arms and making hyena noises.*)

INTERVIEWER :   I beg your pardon?

TRAINER :   Well, he's quite silly looking.

                   If he kept his mouth shut all the time you'd
                   swear he was a Neanderthal.

(*BROTHER makes even louder noises and bobs up and down, keeping
his arms draped loosely over the top of his head and wiggling his
hands.*)

(TRAINER looks at BROTHER and dramatically rolls eyes while turning back to INTERVIEWER.)

TRAINER
(cont.) :   So we have this act, you see.

He mainly spins on his head while I pelt him with little rocks.

(BROTHER bobs up and down even higher and screeches like a hyena.)

The kids love it.

INTERVIEWER :   Oh yeah!

I've seen that act.

It's great!

Lots of action!

I never would have known he was your brother.

TRAINER :   Half-brother.

SFX: CCC Theme Song plays softly

INTERVIEWER :   Yes, yes.

Well, thank you for your time.

This is Grok Boulder for the CCC - Continuous Caveman Coverage.

(Blackout and end of Scene 10.)

SFX: incidental music

Scene 11 - Cave Drill Squad

SETTING:
A blank stage.

AT RISE:
Poster board on easel reads: Cave Drill Squad

(*SQUAD 1 – 7 with spears in the right hand, enter upstage left one at a time, three beats (or steps) apart and end up in a line facing the audience with SQUAD 1 being center stage right and the rest in numerical order to SQUAD 1's left. Each SQUAD grunts when arriving to position.*)

(*SQUAD 1, 3, 5, and 7 march four steps in unison straight forward while simultaneously SQUAD 2, 4 and 6 march four steps in unison straight backwards.*)

(*All grunt and menacingly hold out their spears when they have reached position.*)

(*Everyone marches back to the line position and all again grunt and menacingly hold out their spears when they have reached position.*)

(*SQUAD 2, 4, and 6 march four steps in unison straight forward while simultaneously SQUAD 1, 3, 5, and 7 march four steps in unison straight backwards.*)

(*When they have reached position, all grunt and menacingly hold out their spears.*)

(*Everyone marches back to the line position and all again grunt and menacingly hold out their spears when they have reached position.*)

(*SQUAD 1, 2, and 3 pivot in place to face upstage.*)

(*SQUAD 1, 2, 3, 5, 6, and 7 march clockwise, moving like hands on clock and using SQUAD 4 as the center, until reaching the six o'clock position, grunting all the while. SQUAD 4 marches in place during this.*)

(*Upon reaching the six o'clock position everyone holds up their spear high in the air and grunts loudly.*)

(SQUAD 5, 6 and 7 pivot in place to face stage left while simultaneously SQUAD 1, 2 and 3 pivot in place to face stage right. SQUAD 4 continues to face the audience.)

(SQUAD 1, 2, 3, 5, 6, and 7 march counterclockwise, grunting all the while, and return to line position. SQUAD 4 marches in place during this.)

(SQUAD 5, 6 and 7 upon reaching line position, pivot in place to face the audience.)

(Everyone again grunts loudly and raises their spear high in the air.)

(SQUAD 7 turns and marches to exit upstage left.)

(SQUAD 6 waits three beats, then turns and marches to exit upstage left.)

(SQUAD 5 waits three beats, then turns and marches to exit upstage left.)

(SQUAD 4 waits three beats, then turns and marches to exit upstage left.)

(SQUAD 3 waits three beats, then turns and marches to exit upstage left.)

(SQUAD 2 waits three beats, then turns and marches to exit upstage left.)

(SQUAD 1 waits three beats, then turns and marches to exit upstage left.)

(Blackout and end of Scene 11.)

SFX: incidental music

Scene 12 - The Missing Link 3

SETTING:
GROUP ONE is seated on the floor center stage right. GROUP TWO is seated on the floor center stage left. Both groups have their backs to each other and everyone is acting bored.

AT RISE:
Poster board on easel reads: The Missing Link

(*TV HANDLER enters upstage right carrying a TV on a tray stand. Places the TV and its stand center stage facing the audience. With flair, turns it on and then sits on the floor to watch it, back to the audience.*)

(*GROUP ONE and GROUP TWO one by one notice the TV and get up and go sit down in front of it until they are all sitting together very close and looking only at the TV.*)

(*Blackout and end of Scene 12.*)

SFX: incidental music

Scene 13 - Ice Age Pizza

NOTE: Pleistocene (pronounced PLY-stoh-seen)
NOTE: Precambrian (pronounced pree-KAAHM-bree-ahn)

SETTING:
Center stage sits a table covered with a red-checkered tablecloth. On the table are a tumbler, jelly jar, soda bottle and ginkgo leaves. SMILODON and SCIMITAR both wear puffy chef hats and stand behind the table.

AT RISE:
Poster board on easel reads: Ice Age Pizza

SMILODON :   Welcome, welcome, welcome to Pleistocene Ice Age Pizza — where Cro-Magnons can have it their way!

SCIMITAR :   Yes, we have all your Fossil Favorites here at Pleistocene Pizza.

SMILODON :   Try our Paleolithic Pizza Supreme with Precambrian portobellos, bison bits and our own celebrated tomato grub sauce.

SCIMITAR :   Wash it all down using one of these —

(*lifts tumbler with right hand*)

                    — nifty Triassic Tumblers for the adults or —

(*lifts jelly jar with left hand*)

                    — one of our Jurassic Jelly Jars for the kids.

                    All filled with our salivatin' —

(*motions to soda*)

                    — Stone Age Soda made from —

(*puts down jelly jar and tumbler and holds up leaves*)

                    — real ginkgo leaves.

SMILODON :   And those Mammoth Munchies are on your
               rock at all times.

BOTH :   They're car-bon-niferous!

SMILODON :   Not in the mood for pizza?

               Well, have a Mastodon Steak with a fried
               Pterodactyl Wing on the side.

SCIMITAR :   Or how about a little Sabertooth Sushi?

SMILODON :   If it's your birthday, we'll send a Cenozoic
               Cheesecake Special right to your rock at no
               extra charge.

               You heard me, No Extra Charge!

SCIMITAR :   Can't come to us?

BOTH :   We'll come to you!

*(NEANDERTHAL ONE enters upstage left holding up a pizza box
while NEANDERTHAL TWO enters upstage right holding up a pizza
box. Both start slowly moving downstage, variously poking a finger in
their ear and/or making a show of scratching the side of their butt.)*

SMILODON :   No matter how small your order, we'll send a
               Neanderthal to your door before you can spell
               "EPOCH".

SCIMITAR :   And remember, we use no primates in our
               cooking.

SMILODON :   That's Pleistocene Ice Age Pizza —

BOTH :   Where Cro-magnons can have have it their way!

(Blackout and end of Scene 13.)

SFX: incidental music

Scene 14 - Cave Triathlon

SETTING:
GAMMA and FRIEND stand center stage. ORG is offstage.

AT RISE:
Poster board on easel reads: Cave Triathlon

GAMMA :   I don't know. I just can't stand it anymore.

FRIEND :   Why?

            What's the matter?

GAMMA :   It's Org.

            He's completely devoted to the triathlon for the Annual
            Caveman Games.

ORG :
(*offstage*) Honey?

            I can't find my spear!

GAMMA :
(*yelling back to him*)

            It's at the back of the cave, next to the potion ledge.

FRIEND :   Triathlon?

            I thought all he wanted to do was run faster than anyone.

            What's the triathlon?

GAMMA :   Spear tossing, mammoth riding and speed skinning.

            Yesterday one of the mammoths picked Org up and threw
            him into the tar pit.

            He was a mess!

            Said it was all his fault for not waiting until she had her
            back turned.

GAMMA
(cont.) :   But who gets to clean his skin after that?

                   Me!

ORG :
(*offstage*)   Honey?

                   The hyena's pulling at the baby again.

GAMMA :
(*yelling back to him*)

                   So poke him with your spear —

SFX: baby cries out offstage

                   — the hyena, not the baby!

FRIEND :   Well, you do have plenty of skins.

                   Why don't you throw that one out and give him a new
                   one?

GAMMA :   Because it's his lucky skin, can you believe it?

                   And of course we have plenty of skins what with him
                   speed skinning all the time.

                   This place reeks of them.

                   I never wanted cavewall-to-cavewall carpeting, much
                   less the stinkiest cave in the area.

FRIEND :   So what're you gonna do?

GAMMA :   I don't know.

                   Maybe when he's practicing his spear tossing I'll
                   volunteer to help and pretend that he hit me with it.

                   That'll give him a scare!

GAMMA
(cont.) :   And then he'll have to take care of me instead of training day and night.

FRIEND :   Don't you think he'll catch on?

GAMMA :   Org?

Naw.

ORG :
(*offstage*)   Honey?

Do we have any moss for my tar rash?

GAMMA :
(*yelling back to him*)

Be right there!

(*turning back to FRIEND*)

That man is clueless.

Well, gotta go now.

FRIEND :   Bye.

(*Blackout and end of Scene 14.*)

SFX: incidental music

Scene 15 - Measuring Dinosaurs

SETTING:
PROFESSOR wearing too large glasses and INTERVIEWER are both
seated downstage right at a table with the CCC stegosaurus as the
centerpiece.

AT RISE:
Poster board on easel reads: Measuring Dinosaurs

INTERVIEWER : So, Professor Tally, I understand you've been
measuring dinosaurs for a long time now.

PROFESSOR : Yes, quite some time.

INTERVIEWER : What problems did you initially foresee?

PROFESSOR : Well, my main concern was keeping them still.

It's hard to measure something when it's
moving.

INTERVIEWER : But aren't dinosaurs extinct?

PROFESSOR : Quite.

So that made my theory even more
understandable.

INTERVIEWER : What theory is that?

PROFESSOR : Dead things do not move around very much.

INTERVIEWER : I see.

What are the average sizes of dinosaurs?

PROFESSOR : Oh, they come in economy, small, medium,
large, really large and really really large.

INTERVIEWER : Those don't sound like very accurate
measurements.

PROFESSOR :   Well, it's hard to be accurate when you can't see the end of the tape measure, now isn't it?

By the time the tape has reached the other end of most dinosaurs it's really hard to see.

So I sort of —

(*sniffs, then pushes up glasses*)

— wing it.

INTERVIEWER :   Why don't you lay the tape down and walk to the other end and read it that way?

PROFESSOR :   I had thought of that, but I think it would be a bit dangerous, don't you?

INTERVIEWER :   I don't understand.

PROFESSOR :   Well, I don't know about you, but I certainly don't want to stand next to the rear end of a dinosaur.

You never know what it might —

(*sniffs, then pushes up glasses*)

— smell like.

INTERVIEWER :   But they're extinct. They —

PROFESSOR :   Precisely my point.

And what made them extinct?

INTERVIEWER :   Excuse me?

PROFESSOR :   It could have been something they ate, now couldn't it?

SFX: CCC Theme Song plays softly

(*PROFESSOR smiles real big and pushes up glasses.*)

INTERVIEWER :   Yes, well, thank you.

                  This has been a most interesting interview.

                  This is Minka Mook for the CCC - Continuous
                  Caveman Coverage.

(Blackout and end of Scene 15.)

SFX: incidental music

Scene 16 - Dinosaur Surgery

SETTING:
PATIENT lies on a bench center stage, covered with a sheet up to the neck. Behind the patient sits a box containing the surgeons' props. Downstage right sit MOTHER and FATHER on two chairs. FATHER is silently weeping into his hands; MOTHER is silently comforting him.

AT RISE:
Poster board on easel reads: Dinosaur Surgery

(SURGEON ONE enters upstage right, looking very efficient, and approaches PATIENT.)

SURGEON ONE :   Yes, now, let's see.

Everything seems to be in order.

Yes.

That's good.

Let's see what this dinosaur has been eating lately that's gotten it into our hospital for surgery.

(reaches down and pulls a cardboard cut-out city out of the box)

Ah yes, the Lost City of Atlantis.

We've been wondering where it had gone missing.

(SURGEON ONE exits with the city upstage left while SURGEON TWO enters upstage right.)

SURGEON TWO :   Oh, I know all this must hurt you so much and we're doing our best to make you comfortable.

You've been over-eating lately and that's why you're here and we're doing our best to make you comfortable.

So let's see now what's in your stomach that's making you feel so bad.

SURGEON TWO
(cont.) :
(*reaches down and pulls out a pair of tennis shoes*)

> Oh my! I hope you didn't eat the owner all in one bite!

(*SURGEON TWO exits upstage left with the shoes while SURGEON THREE enters upstage right.*)

SURGEON THREE : Hey!

> It's your lucky day!

> You have me as a surgeon and I'm one of the best in the business.

> No one dies on my shift, I can tell you that.

> Now let's have a look here.

(*reaches down and pulls out a skateboard*)

> Wow!

> Look what rolled your way.

> Well, I'll just have to send this to the lab to see if it's growing in any way.

(*SURGEON THREE exits upstage left with the skateboard while SURGEON FOUR enters upstage right, sneezing all over the place.*)

SURGEON FOUR :
(*sneezing into both hands*)

> Achoo!

(*looks at sneeze-covered hands, does not wipe them off, and shrugs*)

> Oh well.

(*reaches down and pulls out a bag of cookies*)

Cookies!

(*SURGEON FOUR excitedly goes upstage center and is joined by SURGEON ONE, TWO and THREE. They pretend to eat the cookies.*)

(*FATHER starts crying loudly.*)

MOTHER :   There, there, honey.

Our baby will be okay.

(*FATHER keeps weeping loudly.*)

MOTHER :   Honey?

(*FATHER keeps weeping loudly.*)

MOTHER :
(*a little louder*)   Honey?

(*FATHER keeps weeping loudly.*)

MOTHER :
(*even louder*)   Honey?

(*FATHER keeps weeping loudly.*)

MOTHER :
(*screaming*)   SHUUUUUT-UUUUUUP!

(*FATHER freezes silent and falls stiffly to the floor.*)

MOTHER :
(*very calmly*)   Thank you.

(*Blackout and end of Scene 16.*)

SFX: incidental music

Scene 17 - Dinosaur Minuette

AT RISE:
Poster board on easel reads: Dinosaur Minuette

Choreograph your own minuette and use the dinosaur hobbyhorses. We used Bach's Minuette in G. Go to the Kranky Kids website if you want to see how we did it.

(Blackout and end of Scene 17.)

SFX: incidental music

Scene 18 - Cave Fashion Designer

SETTING:
INTERVIEWER and FABRICO (wearing a fancy scarf) are both seated downstage right at a table with the CCC stegosaurus as the centerpiece.

AT RISE:
Poster board on easel reads: Cave Fashion Designer

INTERVIEWER :   Today we are happy to have Fabrico, a first class caveman fashion designer.

Tell us, is it hard to design for the average caveman?

FABRICO :   Oh yes, it's extremely hard.

It's all because of their bad posture, you know.

It makes it very hard to get any good looking effects when you drape the fabric.

And let's face it, draping is IN, very very IN.

INTERVIEWER :   What sort of material do you use?

FABRICO :   Well now, that is a good question!

Most cavemen are hooked on wearing skins from animals.

But here in our cave we're weaving like mad.

And let me tell you, you can do a lot more for the average caveman with woven fabric.

For one thing it doesn't clash so much.

INTERVIEWER :   Clash?

FABRICO :   Positively, my dear.

Sometimes the caveman is hairier than the beast he's wearing.

FABRICO
(cont.) :   A real eyesore.

Of course, we do run into that problem from
another direction, which is why I discourage the
use of very light fabrics.

INTERVIEWER :   Because?

FABRICO :   Because then all their hair pokes through!

I mean, really, there is nothing worse than
seeing a shirt literally stuck to the caveman
who's wearing it, you know what I mean?

By the way, where did you get this perky little
number you have on?

INTERVIEWER :   Oh, this?

It's just something I picked up from Skins-R-
Us.

FABRICO :   Really?

It's quite good on you.

Not a lot of cavemen can get away with the
Woolly Mammoth look.

INTERVIEWER :   Why, thank you.

Any tips for our viewers?

FABRICO :   Yes, stay away from that extinct stuff.

It's cheap and flimsy.

Stay simple and accessorize, accessorize,
accessorize!

Oh, and next season we're introducing
something brand new — they're called SHOES!

INTERVIEWER :   Shoes?

FABRICO :   Yes, you wear them on your feet.

                  Trust me, everyone is going to just love them.

                  We would have introduced them this season but we haven't figured out whether one, or two, will work best.

                  We're still in the tripping stage, you see.

                  Models are plummeting to the floor right and left.

                  It's a mess!

                  But, oh well, what can one do?

SFX: CCC Theme Song plays softly

INTERVIEWER :   Yes, well, I'm certain our viewers will be looking forward to 'shoes'.

                  Thank you again.

                  This is Tak Alot for the CCC - Continuous Caveman Coverage.

(Blackout and end of Scene 18.)

SFX: incidental music

Scene 19 - The Missing Link 4

SETTING:
Center stage right ONE and TWO are struggling to lift a boulder.

AT RISE:
Poster board on easel reads: The Missing Link

(*ONE and TWO grunt and struggle, trying to lift a boulder.*)

(*THREE enters upstage left. Looks at the other two, looks at the audience and shrugs. Then joins the other two and together they all lift the boulder.*)

(*Blackout and end of Scene 19.*)

SFX: incidental music

Scene 20 - Cave Artist

SETTING:
INTERVIEWER and DOUBLE HELIX stand center stage.

AT RISE:
Poster board on easel reads: Cave Artist

INTERVIEWER :   We are speaking with Double Helix, the cave clan's Artist in Residence.

Your work is very well known.

DOUBLE HELIX :   Of course it is.

There's no other work like it.

INTERVIEWER :   Where do you find your inspiration?

DOUBLE HELIX :   Find?

Find?!

You don't find inspiration!

You either have it, or you don't.

And I have it.

INTERVIEWER :   I see.

Your subject matter has caused quite a stir lately.

Some critics say you've gone off the deep end and are worried about what message your work now represents.

DOUBLE HELIX :   Oh, tosh.

I really don't know what all the fuss is about.

All I did was rearrange a few animal parts.

INTERVIEWER :   Yes, but you put the heads of mammoths on the bodies of monkeys.

And you've painted birds with the claws of a sabertooth tiger on several cave walls!

DOUBLE HELIX :   And they look wonderful!

It's time we thought of our world as one big arrangement just waiting, begging to be rearranged.

INTERVIEWER :   How so?

DOUBLE HELIX :   Well, take for example my friend who is a sculptor.

Now he's doing some very interesting work out in the mountains.

He's rearranging the bones of dead animals.

Absolutely fascinating, all the combinations of line and texture he's able to capture.

The flow of each piece.

If you look at my paintings you get the same feeling.

SFX: low, thundering rumble noise starts

INTERVIEWER :   And what feeling is that?

DOUBLE HELIX :   Of change!

CHANGE!

Can't you feel it?

It's happening every moment, every instant, every —

(*starts shaking as if the ground is moving*)

DOUBLE HELIX
(cont.) :   — what's that?

INTERVIEWER :
(*also starts shaking as if the ground is moving*)

What?

DOUBLE HELIX :
(*shakes even more*)   The ground just moved.

Didn't you feel it?

SFX: low, thundering rumble noise gets louder

INTERVIEWER :
(*also shakes even more*)

Y-y-y-y-yes, I can feel it now!

SFX: thundering rumble noise gets much louder

DOUBLE HELIX :
(*yelling and bouncing about*)

You SEE!

You SEE!

CHANGE!

CHANGE!

INTERVIEWER :
(*yelling and bouncing about*)

Thank you!

This is, this is —

INTERVIEWER
and DOUBLE HELIX :
(*falling to the ground*)

WUUU-OOOOOO-AAAAAAAAA!

(*Blackout and end of Scene 20.*)

SFX: incidental music

Scene 21 - The Invention of Chowder

SETTING:
TUNIC and SANDAL, each holding a mic, stand center stage. The rest of the CAST stand behind them with signs in their right hands reading CHOW and signs in their left hands reading DER.

AT RISE:
Poster board on easel reads: The Invention of Chowder

SFX: low crowd sounds on a PA system

(CAST makes various low crowd sounds, also.)

TUNIC :   Yes, ladies and gentlemen, we're here for a real knock-down-drag-out.

SANDAL :   No kidding, Tunic.

             Tonight we have The Chows of Kennebunk bringing in their contestant — a Giant Lobster from the northern Atlantic.

             And the Ders of Anchorage with a Monster King Crab from the northern Pacific.

TUNIC :   Quite a combo for fighting it out in the Grand Culinary Arena, I must say.

SANDAL :   Yes, and all this to take place over a giant cauldron of boiling water and heavy cream for added excitement and entertainment.

TUNIC :   Oh look, the cheerleaders from the Chow camp are throwing some butter into the pot.

SANDAL :   Notice the Der mascots waving their ceremonial garlands of mace and then tossing them into the cauldron also.

TUNIC :   I understand that the Giant Lobster and King Crab will be pelted with potatoes and onions while clawing each other.

SANDAL :   Yes, to see if they lose their balance.

Part of the fun, Tunic.

All part of the fun.

TUNIC :   Okay, folks.

Well, the fight is about to begin.

REFEREE :   Attention!

Attention everyone.

Quiet please!

Thank you.

And now, Giant Lobster of the Chows versus Monster King Crab of the Ders!

SFX: whistle blowing

TUNIC :   Wow, what a tussle.

The King Crab has whipped some cayenne pepper into the lobster's eyes.

SANDAL :   And the lobster just gave the King a taste of his own medicine with claw full of Kosher salt to the gills.

TUNIC :   What a decapod!

This is thrilling!

SANDAL :   And just listen to the crowd!

CAST :
(*leaning right and raising the CHOW signs*)

Chow!

CAST
(cont.) :
(*lowering the CHOW signs, leaning left and raising the DER signs*)

>Der!

(*lowering the DER signs, leaning right and raising the CHOW signs*)

>Chow!

(*lowering the CHOW signs, leaning left and raising the DER signs*)

>Der!

SANDAL :   Oh, no!

>It looks like they've both fallen into the cauldron together!

SFX: splashing sounds

TUNIC :   But the crowd doesn't seem to care!

>Listen!

CAST :
(*raising both signs and shaking them while yelling*)

>Chow-Der!

>Chow-Der!

>Chow-Der!

SFX: lame vocal music intro

(*Entire cast gathers and sings together.*)

EVERYONE :
(*singing and clapping in time*)

>The lobster fell in

EVERYONE
(cont.) :   and the outcome was grim,

for the cauldron it was rather hot.

Chow-Der!

The crab then did stumble,

he fell and he tumbled

And the lobster and crab are now not.

Chow-Der!

(*Blackout and end of Scene 21.*)

SFX: incidental music

NOTE: Alternate Cave Song version (if desired):

EVERYONE :
(*singing and clapping in time*)

The cavemen screamed louder

"We invented chowder!"

When a lobster and dinosaur fought.

Chow-der!

The lobster fell in

And the ref said "He wins!"

And now we like chowder a lot!

Chow-der!

Scene 22 - The Extinction of Dinosaurs

SETTING:
A blank stage.

AT RISE:
Poster board on easel reads: The Extinction of Dinosaurs

SFX: music intro

(*The dinosaurs enter one-by-one casually walking to their positions.*)

(*TYRANNOSAURUS REX enters upstage right and goes to center stage.*)

(*PROTOCERATOPS enters upstage left and goes to downstage center.*)

(*DILOPHOSAURUS enters upstage right and goes to downstage right.*)

(*CORYTHOSAURUS enters upstage left and goes to upstage center.*)

(*CHASMOSAURUS enters upstage right and goes to center stage right.*)

(*ANKYLOSAURUS enters upstage left and goes to center stage left.*)

(*PARASAUROLOPHUS enters upstage right and walks up to DILOPHOSAURUS.*)

PARASAUROLOPHUS :
(*very breathy*)   Huuuh-hi-i-i-i.

(*DILOPHOSAURUS waves the bad breath away and falls to the floor dead.*)

(*PARASAUROLOPHUS looks confused and then goes to CHASMOSAURUS.*)

PARASAUROLOPHUS :
(*very breathy*)   Huuuh-hi-i-i-i.

(*CHASMOSAURUS grabs its nose and falls to the floor dead.*)

(*PARASAUROLOPHUS looks confused again and then goes to CORYTHOSAURUS.*)

PARASAUROLOPHUS :
(*very breathy*)   Huuuh-hi-i-i-i.

(*CORYTHOSAURUS waves the bad breath away and falls to the floor dead.*)

(*PARASAUROLOPHUS looks confused again, shrugs and then goes to ANKYLOSAURUS.*)

PARASAUROLOPHUS :
(*very breathy*)   Huuuh-hi-i-i-i.

(*ANKYLOSAURUS starts coughing and falls to the floor dead.*)

(*PARASAUROLOPHUS looks confused again, shakes head and then goes to PROTOCERATOPS.*)

PARASAUROLOPHUS :
(*very breathy*)   Huuuh-hi-i-i-i.

(*PROTOCERATOPS gasps loudly and falls to the floor dead.*)

(*PARASAUROLOPHUS looks confused again, shakes head, shrugs and then goes to TYRANNOSAURUS REX.*)

PARASAUROLOPHUS :
(*very breathy*)   Huuuh-hi-i-i-i?

(*TYRANNOSAURUS REX clutches its throat and falls to the floor dead.*)

(*PARASAUROLOPHUS blows its own breath into its hand, inhales and, with lots of melodrama, falls to the floor dead.*)

(*After three beats, everyone sits up.*)

EVERYONE :   It's the beginning of the Cenozoic Era
                              with the invention of —

(*holding up their bottles of mouthwash*)

                              — mouthwash!

(*Blackout. End of play.*)

SFX: incidental music

COPYRIGHT

original script
©1999 Lishka DeVoss/Kranky Kids®

ebook script (revised with props added)
©2023 Lishka DeVoss/Kranky Kids®
ISBN-978-1-63441-018-2

paperback script ©2023 Lishka DeVoss/Kranky Kids®
ISBN-978-1-63441-019-9

All rights reserved.

For information contact:

Toad & Fox

Publishers

www.toadfox.com

About Kranky Kids®

Kranky Kids makes educational resources and programs.
Most are available for free at krankykids.com.

Kranky Kids has also been creating and producing original
stage, radio and video productions since 1995.

Lishka DeVoss is the primary author/illustrator.

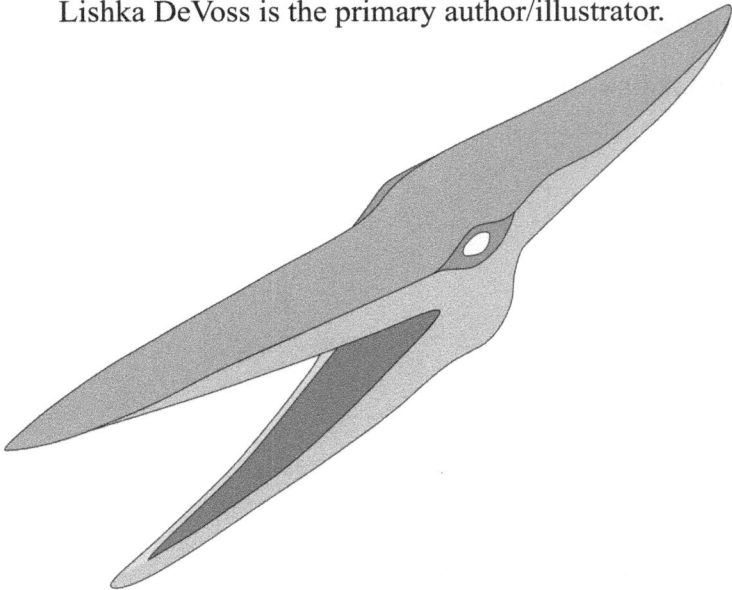

www.ingramcontent.com/pod-product-compliance
Lightning Source LLC
Chambersburg PA
CBHW070518030426
42337CB00037B/2532